Muffins

FAST AND FANTASTIC

Susan Reimer

CHERRY TREE PUBLICATIONS

Muffins: Fast and Fantastic

Published by Cherry Tree Publications, Edinburgh
Visit themuffinbook.uk

Photography by Caroline Trotter

Design by Alison King

I would also like to thank Lydia, Jamie, Brenda, Gill, and all my taste testers for their helpful input.

British Library Cataloguing in Publication Data
Data available

ISBN 978 0 9528858 49

First published in Great Britain 1996 (ISBN 0 9528858 0 8)
Second edition 1999 (ISBN 0 9528858 1 6)
Third edition 2001 (ISBN 0 9528858 2 4)
Third edition, revised 2008 (ISBN 978 0 9528858 3 2)

Printed in the UK by Bell & Bain Ltd

CONTENTS

INTRODUCTION

Life is full of surprises. When *Muffins: Fast and Fantastic* was first published in 1996, I never could have guessed it would still be in print twenty years on. Back then, American muffins were hardly known in Britain, but people were curious about this new food appearing in cafés. It turned out to be the perfect moment for *Muffins* to appear on the scene.

Today, muffins are ubiquitous. They seem to be appearing in all corners of the globe, which testifies to their adaptability and appeal. With this global context in mind, I set myself the challenge of updating *Muffins* for a new generation of bakers.

This edition includes 58 recipes, with over 25 exciting new flavours alongside old favourites. There is plenty of choice for everyone. The wide range of batters includes milk, yogurt, buttermilk, sour cream, juice, and purées—combined with a variety of fruits, vegetables, nuts, oats, and chocolate. With the extensive testing that's gone into creating these recipes, I'm confident you're going to enjoy them!

This current chapter of the *Muffins* story has also taken an unexpected turn. While living in Africa for a time, I was surprised to find that bread flour could make excellent muffins, which naturally sparked a new set of experiments when I returned to the UK. Sure enough, 'strong' bread flour actually produced a better muffin than 'plain' cake flour, superior in both rising and texture. In fact, I had to laugh as I realized I had come full circle: strong bread flour is similar to 'all-purpose' flour—the flour of choice in Canada and the United States, where muffins originated.

(Please read notes on flour, page 12.)

Having a background in public health nursing, I'm always keen to promote healthy eating. But having raised a family, I also know the importance of making food that tastes good! The muffins in this book are nutritionally well-balanced with an emphasis on natural flavours and wholesome goodness.

Given our current understanding of fat and sugar, fat no longer takes the blame for many health issues. Dietary fat is essential for maintaining good health but it needs to be kept in balance. So it's good to know that most of the muffins in this book have only 1½ teaspoons vegetable oil per muffin. Toppings and fillings are extra, of course.

The World Health Organization recommends that sugar

consumption be restricted to a maximum of 30 grams of 'free' sugar per day for adults. This is about 6 level teaspoons of added sugar. You'll be happy to know that most of the muffins in this book have less than 1½ level teaspoons of sugar per muffin. By comparison, most commercial muffins contain 4–5 teaspoons of sugar. My hope is that you'll find the natural flavours of these muffins so delicious, you won't want to increase the sugar! But if you do prefer them sweeter, you can simply nudge the sugar up.

It's worth noting that, historically, muffins were seen as a breakfast quick bread, and were served split and buttered. You might want to consider this when evaluating the sweetness of a muffin, as muffins are not meant to be sweet like cake.

For those who are interested in food history, the earliest recorded muffin recipes can be found in late nineteenth century American cookery books, around the time that baking powder was first developed. It wasn't long before recipes spread north to Canada as well. This type of muffin should not be confused with the flat yeast-leavened 'English muffin' which is entirely different.

Muffins are also part of my own story. During my childhood in the 1960s in Canada, bran muffins were a common snack food in our home. Then, in the 1970s, my mother came across a little book that introduced us to the idea that muffin flavours could extend beyond bran! By the 1980s, muffin-making had become a routine part of my life, baking each week to

enjoy fresh, as well as stocking the freezer for snacks and lunch-boxes.

However, after emigrating to the UK with my husband and two small children in 1993, baking became a frustration as my favourite recipes from Canada flopped time and again for no apparent reason. That sparked the start of my kitchen experiments and the discovery that British plain flour was significantly different from North American all-purpose flour. And so began the *Muffins* story, introducing muffins to the British kitchen.

The technique for making muffins is quick and simple but very different from other forms of baking. To ensure success, please take time to read the following notes about method and ingredients before you begin.

THE MUFFIN METHOD

PREPARATION

All the recipes in this book are designed to produce twelve standard-size muffins although they will reach different heights depending on ingredients. A standard muffin cup is 7cm across the top and 3cm deep. As a guide for other sizes, these recipes will make approximately 36 mini muffins or six jumbo size.

Always read the recipe before you begin, as some require advance preparation. Also, it is very important for muffins to bake in a *preheated* oven to achieve correct rising and texture. A large oven will take about 15 minutes to preheat correctly, so always turn on the oven at the start. Next, prepare the muffin tray by inserting paper cases or by greasing with a solid vegetable fat. At this point, you can gather all the ingredients for the recipe and do any special preparation such as chopping and grating.

NOTES ON MEASURING

Accurate measurements are essential for baking, so you will need standardized measuring spoons, a measuring jug, and weigh scales.

All spoon measures are level:

1 tablespoon = 15ml
1 teaspoon = 5ml

Liquid measurements in a jug should be made at eye-level for accuracy. A flexible spatula (bowl scraper) should be used when transferring liquids and batter.

Be careful to use weigh scales for weight measures given in grams (g), and a measuring jug for volume measures given in millilitres (ml).

Although some electronic weigh scales give an option of measuring volume, they are not actually converting weight to volume. They are relying on the fact that many ingredients, like milk and water, have matching volume/weight measures: 100ml milk weighs 100g. However this is not the case for all ingredients. For example, 100ml vegetable oil weighs 90g.

As Canadians and Americans are accustomed to measuring all ingredients by volume, approximate cup measures have been included for dry ingredients. Cup measures for flour are given on page 128. In addition, metric and imperial conversions are provided on page 127.

MIXING

For each recipe, you will prepare two mixtures: dry and wet (with sugar). The dry ingredients should be sifted together to ensure an even distribution of the raising agent. If you don't have a sieve, use a fork to do this. The wet mixture is always mixed with a fork.

The wet and dry mixtures must be kept separate until just before baking, as liquid activates the raising agent.

When the oven has reached the correct temperature, you are ready to mix the batter. At this point, do a last minute check to see that you have added all the ingredients.

Using a flexible spatula, scrape all of the wet mixture into the dry, and then use an ordinary metal dessert spoon to combine the ingredients. Don't beat the batter, but mix briefly and efficiently with the aim of moistening all the flour in about 20 seconds. Scrape the bottom and sides of the bowl with the spoon while you are mixing, to bring in any dry flour. (This is where a metal spoon is more effective than a wooden one.) Avoid stirring round and round, and do not over stir. As soon as you see that all the flour has been moistened and the mixture looks relatively uniform (with lumps), stop mixing. Ignore the lumpy appearance, and immediately spoon the batter into the muffin cups.

Flour varies in its capacity to absorb liquid, so small adjustments to the amount of liquid might be necessary. Most muffin batters should be neither stiff nor thin, but should be able to drop off the spoon in loose globs.

1   Sift the flour, raising agent, and salt together for even distribution.

2   Beat the egg with a fork until frothy, about 10 seconds. Stir in the sugar.

3   Continue to add the other ingredients as specified. Keep the wet and dry mixtures separate until the oven has reached the correct temperature—about 15 minutes for a large oven.

4   Pour all of the wet mixture into the dry mixture. Scrape with a rubber spatula to retain all the liquid.

5   Using a metal dessert spoon, combine the wet and dry mixtures quickly and briefly with the aim of moistening all the flour in about 20 seconds. Do not over stir! The batter should appear lumpy but evenly mixed. Avoid stirring round and round. Instead mix efficiently using a minimum of strokes, scraping the bottom and sides of the bowl with the spoon to bring in any dry flour.

6   Immediately spoon the lumpy batter into the muffin cases and bake in a moderately hot preheated oven.

BAKING

Muffins must be put into a moderately hot preheated oven so they can start to rise within five minutes. Standard size muffins should be well-risen and lightly browned in approximately 20 minutes. At this point, open the oven door and touch one of the tops lightly with your finger. If your finger leaves an indent or the muffins look pale, continue baking another 2–3 minutes and check again. Muffins are done when they hold their shape and have a good colour. Some tops feel firm when baked while others feel a bit soft or springy. The important thing is that they should keep their shape after the touch test. Avoid over-baking as this dries out the muffins.

Several factors can prevent good rising, such as inadequate preheating, wrong oven temperature, stale or incorrect raising agents, and poor wet/dry balance. If the muffins spread out over the pan during baking, it usually means the batter is too wet. If the muffins are small and dense, the batter is too dry.

With a fan oven, you might find the muffin tops are distorted or flat. This is due to the hot fan air drying the tops too quickly before they have a chance to rise properly. A topping, or even a pinch of sprinkled sugar, will help to prevent this.

COOLING AND STORING

By allowing the muffins to cool several minutes after baking, they will come out of the cases, or greased pan, more easily. Low-sugar muffins have a tendency to stick to paper cases. You can slip a knife just inside the case, and run it around the muffin to release it.

Due to the low sugar and fat content of these recipes, they are best served on the day of baking. Ideally, any leftover muffins should be frozen on the same day in airtight bags to maintain freshness. If freezing is not possible, store them in an airtight container and eat within two days. Re-heat to restore freshness.

To thaw a frozen muffin quickly, warm it in a microwave oven for 30–40 seconds at Medium, or in a moderate oven for 5–10 minutes.

KNOW YOUR INGREDIENTS

Each recipe in this book has been carefully crafted to ensure optimum rising, flavour, and texture. If you change the chemistry of the batter, you could end up with something quite different! Having said that, muffins are remarkably adaptable if you understand your ingredients.

FLOUR
This edition marks a significant change in the choice of flour: from British 'plain' flour to 'strong' flour. In Britain, it's assumed that plain cake flour is best for muffins. But in recent years, I've found that strong bread flour makes even better muffins. How can this be? Strong flour is able to absorb more liquid than plain or self-raising flour, which means the final result is more moist.

The high gluten (protein) content of bread flour makes it unsuitable for standard cake batters, as gluten becomes elastic with vigorous stirring or beating. But muffin batter is combined using only a minimum of strokes, so the gluten is not a problem. The result is a well-risen, moist, and delicate muffin.

In North America where muffins originated, 'all-purpose flour' is used. Its 13% protein content is similar to British strong flour. These two flours are interchangeable by weight although there is a slight difference by volume. American cup measures are given on page 128.

When using this book in other countries, you should choose flour with a protein content as close to 13% as possible.

Although strong bread flour is the best option in the UK, plain or self-raising flour can be substituted if necessary, provided the amount of liquid is reduced. Hold back 3 tablespoons and adjust as necessary. With British self-raising flour, omit baking powder from the recipe but do not alter bicarbonate of soda or salt. (Self-raising flour in Britain does not contain salt.)

If you would like to use wholemeal flour, I would recommend a half-and-half combination to maintain a light texture. Even substituting a small amount of wholemeal flour, such as 50g, will increase fibre and nutritional content.

For wheat-free and gluten-free baking, see page 126.

BAKING POWDER AND BICARBONATE OF SODA are not interchangeable! Baking powder contains both acid and alkaline substances which react together to form tiny bubbles when liquid is added. These bubbles expand when heated, causing the batter to rise. Bicarbonate of soda is simply alkaline, and therefore is not a substitute for baking powder.

After extensive testing, I found myself questioning the common practice of using bicarbonate of soda in combination with strongly acidic ingredients. Although soda bread is delicious, its distinctive flavour doesn't suit all baking. Bicarbonate of soda must be used carefully and cautiously to maximize benefits while avoiding unpleasant effects in flavour and colour. Please be careful to use the raising agents exactly as specified in each recipe.

SALT plays a vital role in the chemistry and flavour of baking. The small amount of salt in these recipes should not be omitted! I have fond childhood memories of my mother taking delicious baking out of the oven week by week but, on rare occasions, would hear her groan: 'Oh no, I forgot the salt!' Omission of salt in baking produces sub-standard results—flat flavour along with poor texture and appearance. In addition, the loss of flavour often prompts a boost in sugar to compensate. If you need to reduce salt in your diet, it is better to cut back on processed foods rather than eliminate salt from your baking.

EGG enhances texture, rising, and nutritional value of baked goods. The egg should be beaten with a fork until frothy, about 10 seconds, to ensure even distribution in the batter. You don't want to find a lump of cooked egg in your muffin! These recipes call for a large egg (4 tablespoons). If eggs must be omitted for any reason, increase the liquid by about 3 tablespoons.

SUGAR is used for flavour and texture. In general, muffins should be sweeter than scones but not as sweet as cake. Even savoury muffins benefit from a small amount of sugar.

Every recipe in this book makes 12 standard-size muffins and most batches contain 75–85g sugar. That is 6–7g sugar per muffin

(1¼–1½ level teaspoons) which is considerably less than commercial muffins and most cakes. If you prefer them sweeter, or less sweet, simply adjust the amount of sugar to suit.

For those on sugar-restricted diets, it can be reduced to 1–2 tablespoons per batch which equals ¼–½ teaspoon per muffin. It is normal for low-sugar muffins to sink a little after baking.

Note that it is best to add sugar to the wet ingredients so that it dissolves better in the batter.

FAT is needed for good texture and is, in itself, an important nutrient. Vegetable oil from rapeseed or canola is considered the most suitable oil for baking due to its mild flavour. Vegetable oil produces a light non-greasy texture in muffins, as well as being more economical and easier to use than butter. For some recipes, butter is specified for a particular flavour or method of mixing. A suitable margarine can also be used.

MILK contributes to nutrition, flavour, and texture in baking. It might be worth mentioning that full and semi fat milk and yogurt are not high-fat foods. In fact, they offer significant health benefits over no-fat options. For a dairy-free diet, alternative products such as soya milk can be substituted.

BUTTERMILK is a naturally low fat product and should have a thin pouring consistency with a pleasant tangy flavour. Unfortunately some buttermilk products have a thick yogurt-like consistency and fail to give a desirable result. If you can't find good buttermilk, you can substitute a combination of milk and whole milk yogurt in equal parts.

FRESH FRUIT AND VEGETABLES release liquid into the batter during baking whereas dried fruit absorbs liquid. This should be kept in mind when adapting recipes, as the liquid might need to be adjusted by 1–2 tablespoons.

LEMON JUICE is commonly used for souring milk, supposedly to produce a lighter product. In my experience, the opposite is true. It causes the milk to curdle rather than sour, which means the milk has separated into curds and whey, and the final result is a heavier product. Lemon juice should be added at the final mixing, giving a boost of acidity without curdling the milk. (But be sure to keep it nearby so you don't forget it!)

UNSWEETENED COCOA POWDER is a source of dietary minerals, including iron. Cocoa has a negative reputation because it is usually combined with large amounts of sugar and fat. This book uses reduced sugar and fat. As cocoa mixes best in fat, it should be added to the wet ingredients.

WHEAT BRAN is a rich source of beneficial dietary fibre and nutrients. It can be found in health food shops and some supermarkets. Please note that oat bran differs significantly from wheat bran, and is not a substitute in these recipes.

CHOCOLATE

Chocolate

Chocolate Apricot

Chocolate Beetroot

Chocolate Cheesecake

Chocolate Chip

Chocolate Orange

Chocolate Pear

Chocolate Raspberry

Chocolate Ripple

Cocoa Courgette

Mocha Cheesecake

Mocha Cherry

Chocolate Muffins

250g strong white bread flour*

1½ teaspoons baking powder

½ teaspoon bicarbonate of soda

¼ teaspoon salt

3–4 tablespoons chocolate chips

1 large egg

85–100g white granulated sugar (⅓ – ½ c)

125ml vegetable oil

50g (8 tablespoons) cocoa powder

250ml milk

75ml water

Optional topping: extra chocolate chips
  or grated chocolate

*This is equivalent to American
all-purpose flour.*

1   Preheat a conventional oven to 190°C (375°F), Gas Mark 5, fan oven 170°C. Prepare the muffin pan.

2   In a large bowl, sift together flour, baking powder, bicarbonate of soda, and salt. Add chocolate chips.

3   In a medium-sized bowl, beat egg briskly with a fork. Stir well after each addition: sugar, oil, cocoa, milk, and water.

4   When the oven is ready, pour all of wet mixture into dry. With a metal spoon, mix lightly just until combined and no dry flour is visible, about 20–30 seconds. Do not beat. This batter is thinner than most.

5   Spoon into 12 standard muffin cups. Sprinkle with chocolate. Bake about 20 minutes until done. Do not overbake.

Chocolate Glazed Muffins For a glazed variation, omit chocolate chips. Combine 1 tablespoon cocoa powder with 2 tablespoons melted butter. Add 2 teaspoons warm water and 75g icing sugar (⅔ c). Stir until smooth. This glaze thickens as it cools. Add a few drops of water if necessary. Makes about 1 teaspoon per muffin.

A **double chocolate** treat

Apricots
are **rich in
nutrients**

Chocolate Apricot Muffins

250g strong white bread flour

1½ teaspoons baking powder

½ teaspoon bicarbonate of soda

¼ teaspoon salt

1 large egg

75–85g white granulated sugar (⅓ c)

100ml vegetable oil

35g (6 tablespoons) cocoa powder

250ml milk

50ml water

100g dried apricots, for purée (½ c)

50g dried apricots, diced (¼ c)

Optional: 50g walnuts, chopped (½ c)

1 Preheat a conventional oven to 190°C (375°F), Gas Mark 5, fan oven 170°C. Prepare the muffin pan.

2 For purée: Put 100g diced apricots in a small saucepan with plenty of water to cover. Bring to the boil, reduce heat, cover, and simmer for 10 minutes. Drain. Purée with an electric blender and set aside. Prepare 50g diced apricots.

3 In a large bowl, sift together flour, baking powder, bicarbonate of soda, and salt.

4 In a medium-sized bowl, beat egg briskly with a fork. Stir well after each addition: sugar, oil, cocoa, milk, water, apricot purée, and 50g diced apricots.

5 When the oven is ready, pour all of wet mixture into dry. (Add nuts if using.) With a metal spoon, mix lightly just until combined and no dry flour is visible, about 20 seconds. Do not beat or over stir.

6 Fill cups nearly full. Bake about 20 minutes until done. Makes 12.

Chocolate Beetroot Muffins

275g strong white bread flour

2 teaspoons baking powder

¼ teaspoon bicarbonate of soda

¼ teaspoon salt

3–4 tablespoons chocolate chips

1 large egg

75–85g white granulated sugar (⅓ c)

100ml vegetable oil

50g (8 tablespoons) cocoa powder

200ml buttermilk*

100ml milk

4 tablespoons water

150ml puréed cooked beetroot

Cream Cheese Icing:

50g full fat cream cheese

1 tablespoon soft butter (not melted)

100g icing sugar (¾ c)

¼ teaspoon vanilla extract

1   Boil 2–3 whole small beetroot (minimum 300g total) about 40 minutes until tender. Drain, peel, and purée. Measure 150ml.

2   Preheat a conventional oven to 190°C (375°F), Gas Mark 5, fan oven 170°C. Prepare the muffin pan.

3   In a large bowl, sift together flour, baking powder, bicarbonate of soda, and salt. Add chocolate chips.

4   In a medium-sized bowl, beat egg briskly with a fork. Stir well after each addition: sugar, oil, cocoa, buttermilk, milk, water, and beetroot purée.

5   When the oven is ready, pour wet mixture into dry. Mix lightly with a metal spoon just until combined and no dry flour is visible, about 20 seconds. Do not over stir.

6   Fill cups nearly full. Bake about 20 minutes until done. Makes 12.

7   Stir icing ingredients until smooth. Use the back of the spoon to cream them together.

If you can't find a good thin buttermilk, use a blend of milk and whole milk yogurt, in equal portions.

Flavourful, with **eye-catching** red tops

Chocolate Cheesecake Muffins

250g strong white bread flour

1½ teaspoons baking powder

½ teaspoon bicarbonate of soda

¼ teaspoon salt

1 large egg

75–85g white granulated sugar (⅓ c)

100ml vegetable oil

50g (8 tablespoons) cocoa powder

250ml milk

100ml water

Filling:

150g full fat cream cheese

2 tablespoons white granulated sugar

3 tablespoons coarsely grated
  dark chocolate

Topping: extra grated chocolate

1   Preheat a conventional oven to 190°C (375°F), Gas Mark 5, fan oven 170°C. Prepare the muffin pan.

2   Stir filling ingredients together and set aside. Prepare extra grated chocolate for topping, about 2 tablespoons.

3   In a large bowl, sift together flour, baking powder, bicarbonate of soda, and salt.

4   In a medium-sized bowl, beat egg briskly with a fork. Stir well after each addition: sugar, oil, cocoa, milk, and water.

5   When the oven is ready, pour wet mixture into dry. With a metal spoon, mix lightly just until combined and no dry flour is visible, about 20 seconds. Do not beat or over stir.

6   Put a spoonful of batter into each muffin cup to cover the base. Add a spoonful of filling to each, and then top with remaining batter. Sprinkle with grated chocolate. Bake about 20 minutes until done. Makes 12.

Chocolate Chip Muffins

275g strong white bread flour

2½ teaspoons baking powder

¼ teaspoon bicarbonate of soda

¼ teaspoon salt

75g dark or milk chocolate chips (⅓ c)

1 large egg

60–75g white granulated sugar (¼–⅓ c)

100ml vegetable oil

250ml milk

100g finely chopped sweet red apple (⅔ c)*

Apple adds natural sweetness and a moist texture. To make these without apple, simply substitute 2 tablespoons water.

1 Preheat a conventional oven to 190°C (375°F), Gas Mark 5, fan oven 170°C. Prepare the muffin pan.

2 In a large bowl, sift together flour, baking powder, bicarbonate of soda, and salt. Add chocolate chips.

3 In a medium-sized bowl, beat egg briskly with a fork. Stir in sugar, oil, milk, and apple (or water).

4 When the oven is ready, pour all of wet mixture into dry. With a metal spoon, mix lightly just until combined and no dry flour is visible, about 20 seconds. Do not beat or over stir.

5 Fill cups nearly full. Sprinkle tops with extra chocolate chips if desired. Bake about 20 minutes until lightly browned. Makes 12.

Mandarins add a **fruity sweetness**

Chocolate Orange Muffins

275g strong white bread flour

2 teaspoons baking powder

½ teaspoon bicarbonate of soda

¼ teaspoon salt

3–4 tablespoons chocolate chips

1 large egg

75–85g white granulated sugar (⅓ c)

100ml vegetable oil

30g (5 tablespoons) cocoa powder

2 teaspoons finely grated orange zest
   (of 2 firm juice oranges)

150ml milk

100ml water

2 tablespoons orange juice

150g tinned mandarin orange
   segments,* sliced (⅔ c)

*Tinned mandarin segments are
sweeter and less fibrous than fresh.*

1 Preheat a conventional oven to 190°C (375°F), Gas Mark 5, fan oven 170°C. Prepare the muffin pan.

2 In a large bowl, sift together flour, baking powder, bicarbonate of soda, and salt. Add chocolate chips.

3 In a medium-sized bowl, beat egg briskly with a fork. Stir well after each addition: sugar, oil, cocoa, zest, milk, water, and juice. Prepare mandarin segments but do not add them yet.

4 When the oven is ready, pour all of wet mixture into dry. With a metal spoon, mix lightly just until combined and no dry flour is visible, about 20 seconds. Gently fold in mandarin pieces during the final strokes. Do not over stir.

5 Fill cups nearly full. Bake about 20 minutes until done. Makes 12.

Chocolate Pear Muffins

275g strong white bread flour

1½ teaspoons baking powder

½ teaspoon bicarbonate of soda

¼ teaspoon salt

1 large egg

75–85g white granulated sugar (⅓ c)

100ml vegetable oil

50g (8 tablespoons) cocoa powder

200ml milk

100ml tinned pear juice or water

200g chopped pears, tinned or fresh (1 c)

Optional topping: grated chocolate

1 Preheat a conventional oven to 190°C (375°F), Gas Mark 5, fan oven 170°C. Prepare the muffin pan.

2 In a large bowl, sift together flour, baking powder, bicarbonate of soda, and salt.

3 In a medium-sized bowl, beat egg briskly with a fork. Stir well after each addition: sugar, oil, cocoa, milk, juice/water, and chopped pears.

4 When the oven is ready, pour all of wet mixture into dry. With a metal spoon, mix lightly just until combined and no dry flour is visible, about 20 seconds. Do not beat or over stir.

5 Fill cups nearly full. Sprinkle with grated chocolate, if desired. Bake about 20 minutes until done. Makes 12.

Use tinned pears to **enjoy these year round**

A delicious blend
of **sweet and tart**

Chocolate Raspberry Muffins

250g strong white bread flour

2 teaspoons baking powder

¼ teaspoon bicarbonate of soda

¼ teaspoon salt

1 large egg

75–85g white granulated sugar (⅓ c)

75ml vegetable oil

35g (6 tablespoons) cocoa powder

150ml sour cream (cultured)

150ml milk

3 tablespoons water

150g raspberries, halved or quartered
  (1 c); do not thaw if frozen

Optional topping: grated chocolate

1   Preheat a conventional oven to 190°C (375°F), Gas Mark 5, fan oven 170°C. Prepare the muffin pan.

2   In a large bowl, sift together flour, baking powder, bicarbonate of soda, and salt.

3   In a medium-sized bowl, beat egg briskly with a fork. Stir well after each addition: sugar, oil, cocoa, sour cream, milk, and water. Prepare berries but do not add them yet.

4   When the oven is ready, pour wet mixture into dry. With a metal spoon, mix lightly just until combined and no dry flour is visible, about 20 seconds. Gently fold in berries.

5   Fill cups nearly full. Sprinkle tops with grated chocolate. Bake about 20 minutes until done. Frozen fruit might require an extra 2–3 minutes. Makes 12.

Chocolate Ripple Muffins

275g strong white bread flour

2 teaspoons baking powder

¼ teaspoon bicarbonate of soda

¼ teaspoon salt

1 large egg

60g white granulated sugar (¼ c)

100ml vegetable oil

200ml buttermilk*

100ml milk

2 tablespoons water

Filling:

25g (2 tablespoons) butter

2 tablespoons light brown soft sugar

½ teaspoon ground cinnamon

75g dark chocolate, broken

Topping: coarsely grated chocolate

Optional decoration: 12 pecan halves

1 Preheat a conventional oven to 190°C (375°F), Gas Mark 5, fan oven 170°C. Prepare the muffin pan.

2 Place filling ingredients in a heat-proof bowl over hot water. High heat damages the texture of chocolate. Stir constantly just until melted, and then set aside to cool. Prepare topping.

3 In a large bowl, sift together flour, baking powder, bicarbonate of soda, and salt.

4 In a medium-sized bowl, beat egg briskly with a fork. Stir in sugar, oil, buttermilk, milk, and water.

5 When the oven is ready, pour wet mixture into dry. With a metal spoon, mix lightly just until combined, about 20 seconds. This batter is quite thick. Do not over stir.

6 Drop a spoonful of batter into each cup to cover the base. If the chocolate mixture has thickened, add a few drops of water. Drizzle a spoonful into each cup. Top with remaining batter, grated chocolate, and a pecan. Bake about 20 minutes until lightly browned. Makes 12.

If you can't find a good thin buttermilk, substitute a blend of milk and whole milk yogurt, in equal portions.

Deliciously
sophisticated

Cocoa Courgette Muffins

250g strong white bread flour

2½ teaspoons baking powder

½ teaspoon bicarbonate of soda

¼ teaspoon salt

2 teaspoons ground cinnamon

1 large egg

75–85g light brown soft sugar (⅓ c)

100ml vegetable oil

35g (6 tablespoons) cocoa powder

300g finely grated courgette (1¼ c)

100ml milk

4 tablespoons water

75g raisins or sultanas (½ c)

1 Preheat a conventional oven to 190°C (375°F), Gas Mark 5, fan oven 170°C. Prepare the muffin pan.

2 Peel the courgette (also known as zucchini) and grate finely. As courgette provides most of the liquid, chopping is not adequate.

3 In a large bowl, sift together flour, baking powder, bicarbonate of soda, salt, and cinnamon.

4 In a medium-sized bowl, beat egg briskly with a fork. Stir well after each addition: sugar, oil, cocoa, courgette, milk, water, and raisins.

5 When the oven is ready, pour wet mixture into dry. With a metal spoon, mix lightly just until combined and no dry flour is visible, about 20 seconds. Do not beat or over stir.

6 Fill cups nearly full. Bake about 20 minutes until done. Makes 12.

Mocha Cheesecake Muffins

275g strong white bread flour

1½ teaspoons baking powder

½ teaspoon bicarbonate of soda

¼ teaspoon salt

1 large egg

75–85g white granulated sugar (⅓ c)

100ml vegetable oil

25g (4 tablespoons) cocoa powder

100ml milk

150ml cold water

3 tablespoons instant coffee granules

50ml hot water

Filling:

150g full fat cream cheese

2–3 tablespoons white granulated sugar

1 teaspoon instant coffee granules

Topping: grated dark chocolate

1   Preheat a conventional oven to 190°C (375°F), Gas Mark 5, fan oven 170°C. Prepare the muffin pan.

2   Stir filling ingredients together and set aside. Prepare grated chocolate, about 2 tablespoons.

3   In a large bowl, sift together flour, baking powder, bicarbonate of soda, and salt.

4   In a medium-sized bowl, beat egg briskly with a fork. Stir well after each addition: sugar, oil, cocoa, milk, and cold water. Dissolve coffee granules in 50ml hot water and add to wet mixture.

5   When the oven is ready, pour wet mixture into dry. With a metal spoon, mix lightly just until combined and no dry flour is visible, about 20 seconds. Do not beat or over stir.

6   Put a spoonful of batter into each muffin cup to cover the base. Add a spoonful of filling to each, and then top with remaining batter. Sprinkle with grated chocolate. Bake about 20 minutes until done. Makes 12.

A **classic** combination

Mocha Cherry Muffins

250g strong white bread flour

2 teaspoons baking powder

¼ teaspoon bicarbonate of soda

¼ teaspoon salt

1 large egg

75–85g white granulated sugar (⅓ c)

75ml vegetable oil

35g (6 tablespoons) cocoa powder

150ml sour cream (cultured)

150ml cold water

3 tablespoons instant coffee granules

50ml hot water

150–200g pitted cherries, halved (1–1¼ c)

Light Chocolate Sauce:

2½ teaspoons cornflour (cornstarch)

250ml milk

4 tablespoons white granulated sugar

4 tablespoons cocoa powder

2 tablespoons butter

1 Preheat a conventional oven to 190°C (375°F), Gas Mark 5, fan oven 170°C. Prepare the muffin pan.

2 In a large bowl, sift together flour, baking powder, bicarbonate of soda, and salt.

3 In a separate bowl, beat egg briskly with a fork. Stir well after each addition: sugar, oil, cocoa, sour cream, and cold water. Dissolve coffee granules in 50ml hot water, and add to the wet mixture along with cherries.

4 When the oven is ready, pour wet mixture into dry. With a metal spoon, mix lightly just until combined and no dry flour is visible, about 20–30 seconds.

5 Fill cups nearly full. Bake about 20 minutes until done. Makes 12.

6 For the optional sauce, stir cornflour and cold milk together in a small saucepan until smooth. Add sugar, cocoa, and butter. Place over low heat and stir constantly until smooth and bubbling, about 2 minutes. Remove from heat; do not overheat. Makes 2 tablespoons sauce per muffin.

NUTS AND OATS

Apricot Almond
Butter Pecan
Cinnamon Swirl
Coffee Date Walnut
Cranberry Oat
Fruit 'n' Spice
Granola
Hazelnut and Chocolate
Maple Walnut
Oat Chocolate Chip
Oat Pear
Peanut Butter Oat

Apricot Almond Muffins

275g strong white bread flour

2½ teaspoons baking powder

¼ teaspoon bicarbonate of soda

¼ teaspoon salt

75g flaked almonds (⅔ c)

1 large egg

75–85g light brown soft sugar (⅓ c)

100ml vegetable oil

250ml milk

2 tablespoons water

150g dried apricots (¾ c)

Topping: extra flaked almonds

1 Preheat a conventional oven to 190°C (375°F), Gas Mark 5, fan oven 170°C. Prepare the muffin pan.

2 Soak dried apricots in hot water for about 10 minutes. Drain, and cut into small chunks.

3 Place almonds on a baking sheet, and toast in a preheated oven about 3 minutes, just until lightly browned.

4 In a large bowl, sift together flour, baking powder, bicarbonate of soda, and salt. Add toasted almonds.

5 In a medium-sized bowl, beat egg briskly with a fork. Stir in sugar, oil, milk, water, and chopped apricots.

6 When the oven is ready, pour wet mixture into dry. Mix lightly with a metal spoon just until combined and no dry flour is visible, about 20 seconds. Do not over stir.

7 Fill cups nearly full. Sprinkle with extra untoasted almonds. Bake about 20 minutes until lightly browned. Makes 12.

A **winner**
for flavour
and nutrition

Inspired by the classic
Canadian butter tart

Butter Pecan Muffins

250g strong white bread flour

2 teaspoons baking powder

½ teaspoon bicarbonate of soda

¼ teaspoon salt

1 large egg

60–75g light brown soft sugar (⅓ c)

250ml milk

2 tablespoons water

75g currants or raisins (½ c)*

75g pecans, chopped (⅔ c)

100g butter, melted (½ c)

Topping:

1 tablespoon butter, melted

2 tablespoons light brown soft sugar

40g pecans, chopped (⅓ c)

*Tip: If your dried fruit has become
hard, it can be plumped up by soaking
in hot water for about 10 minutes.*

1 Preheat a conventional oven to 190°C (375°F), Gas Mark 5, fan oven 170°C. Prepare the muffin pan.

2 Combine topping ingredients and set aside.

3 In a large bowl, sift together flour, baking powder, bicarbonate of soda, and salt.

4 In a medium-sized bowl, beat egg briskly with a fork. Add sugar, milk, water, currants, pecans, and butter.

5 When the oven is ready, pour wet mixture into dry. With a metal spoon, mix lightly just until combined and no dry flour is visible, about 20 seconds. Do not over stir. This batter is wetter than most.

6 Fill cups nearly full. Sprinkle with topping. Bake about 20 minutes until lightly browned. Makes 12.

Cinnamon Swirl Muffins

250g strong white bread flour

2 teaspoons baking powder

¼ teaspoon bicarbonate of soda

¼ teaspoon salt

1 large egg

60g white granulated sugar (¼ c)

75ml vegetable oil

150ml milk

150ml sour cream (cultured)

50ml water

Filling and Topping:

2–3 tablespoons light brown soft sugar

100g pecans or walnuts, chopped (¾ c)

2 teaspoons ground cinnamon

1. Preheat a conventional oven to 190°C (375°F), Gas Mark 5, fan oven 170°C. Prepare the muffin pan.

2. Prepare the filling and topping mixture, and set aside. (Nuts can be omitted if preferred.)

3. In a large bowl, sift together flour, baking powder, bicarbonate of soda, and salt.

4. In a medium-sized bowl, beat egg briskly with a fork. Stir in white sugar, oil, milk, sour cream, and water.

5. When the oven is ready, pour wet mixture into dry. With a metal spoon, mix lightly just until combined and no dry flour is visible, about 20 seconds. Do not beat or over stir.

6. Put a spoonful of batter into each muffin cup to cover the base. Distribute half the cinnamon mixture. Spoon out the remaining batter and finish with the other half of the cinnamon mixture. Bake about 20 minutes until lightly browned. Makes 12.

An enticing **sour cream** muffin

Coffee Date Walnut Muffins

275g strong white bread flour

2 teaspoons baking powder

½ teaspoon bicarbonate of soda

¼ teaspoon salt

1 large egg

75–85g light brown soft sugar (⅓ c)

200ml milk

200ml boiling water

3 tablespoons instant coffee granules

150g dried dates, chopped (1 c)

100g butter, melted (½ c)

75g walnuts, chopped (⅔ c)

1　Preheat a conventional oven to 190°C (375°F), Gas Mark 5, fan oven 170°C. Prepare the muffin pan.

2　Dissolve coffee granules in 200ml boiling water. Pour over chopped dates in a bowl, and leave this to soak and cool for 10 minutes. Do not drain. Meanwhile, chop nuts and set aside.

3　In a large bowl, sift together flour, baking powder, bicarbonate of soda, and salt.

4　In a medium-sized bowl, beat egg briskly with a fork. Stir in sugar, milk, cooled coffee/dates, and melted butter.

5　When the oven is ready, pour wet mixture into dry, along with walnuts. Mix lightly with a metal spoon just until combined and no dry flour is visible, about 20 seconds. Do not over stir.

6　Fill cups nearly full. Bake about 20 minutes until golden brown. Makes 12.

Photo: page 38, left

Cranberry Oat Muffins

250g strong white bread flour

2 teaspoons baking powder

¼ teaspoon bicarbonate of soda

¼ teaspoon salt

50g rolled oats (½ c)

1 large egg

75–85g white granulated sugar (⅓ c)

100ml vegetable oil

150ml whole milk yogurt

250ml milk

100g cranberries, chopped (1 c)

1. Preheat a conventional oven to 190°C (375°F), Gas Mark 5, fan oven 170°C. Prepare the muffin pan.

2. In a large bowl, sift together flour, baking powder, bicarbonate of soda, and salt. Add oats.

3. In a medium-sized bowl, beat egg briskly with a fork. Add sugar, oil, yogurt, milk, and cranberries.

4. When the oven is ready, pour wet mixture into dry. With a metal spoon, mix lightly just until combined and no dry flour is visible, about 20 seconds. Do not beat or over stir.

5. Spoon into muffin cups. Sprinkle tops with a pinch of sugar, if desired. Bake about 20 minutes until lightly browned. Makes 12.

Sultana Oat Muffins Replace fresh berries with 100g (⅔ c) dried fruit such as sultanas, raisins, or dried cranberries. Add 1 tablespoon water.

Subtle spices,
warm aromas

Fruit 'n' Spice Muffins

225g strong white bread flour

2 teaspoons baking powder

½ teaspoon bicarbonate of soda

¼ teaspoon salt

1 teaspoon ground cinnamon

½ teaspoon ground cloves

¼ teaspoon ground nutmeg

50g rolled oats (½ c)

1 large egg

75–85g light brown soft sugar (⅓ c)

100ml vegetable oil

250ml milk

2 tablespoons water

100g finely chopped sweet red apple (⅔ c)

50g walnuts, chopped (½ c)

50g raisins (⅓ c)

50g soft dried dates, chopped (⅓ c)

1 Preheat a conventional oven to 190°C (375°F), Gas Mark 5, fan oven 170°C. Prepare the muffin pan.

2 If the dates are hard, soak them first in hot water for about 10 minutes, and then drain. Prepare apple, nuts, raisins, and dates. Set aside.

3 In a large bowl, sift together flour, baking powder, bicarbonate of soda, salt, and spices. Add oats.

4 In a medium-sized bowl, beat egg briskly with a fork. Stir in sugar, oil, milk, water, apple, nuts, raisins, and dates.

5 When the oven is ready, pour wet mixture into dry. With a metal spoon, mix lightly just until combined and no dry flour is visible, about 20 seconds. Do not beat or over stir.

6 Fill cups nearly full. Sprinkle each top with a pinch of brown sugar if desired. Bake about 20 minutes until lightly browned. Makes 12.

Granola Muffins

250g strong white bread flour

2 teaspoons baking powder

¼ teaspoon bicarbonate of soda

¼ teaspoon salt

1 large egg

75–85g white granulated sugar (⅓ c)

100ml vegetable oil

250ml milk

100ml whole milk yogurt

2 tablespoons water

Granola Mix,* cooled

Optional: 3 tablespoons chocolate chips

See opposite page for Granola Mix.

1. Prepare the granola in advance. Preheat the oven to a moderate heat: conventional oven 160°C (325°F), Gas Mark 3, fan oven 140°C. Chop almonds and pecans, and combine with oats and seeds. Stir melted butter and honey together and add to oat mixture, stirring well to coat. Arrange mixture in a circle on a baking sheet, keeping it away from the edges of the pan and about 1 cm deep to avoid scorching. Bake about 15 minutes until lightly golden, stirring every 5 minutes. It will become crunchy after cooling. Set aside 75g (⅔ cup) for topping.

2. Now preheat the oven to 190°C (375°F), Gas Mark 5, fan oven 170°C. Prepare the muffin pan.

3. In a large bowl, sift together flour, baking powder, bicarbonate of soda, and salt. Add chocolate if using.

4. In a medium-sized bowl, beat egg briskly with a fork. Add sugar, oil, milk, yogurt, and water.

5. When the oven is ready, pour wet mixture into dry, along with granola. (Remember to reserve topping.) With a metal spoon, mix lightly just until combined and no dry flour is visible, about 20 seconds. Do not beat or over stir.

6. Spoon into cups. Sprinkle with reserved granola. Bake about 20 minutes until lightly browned. Makes 12.

Granola Mix:

50g almonds, chopped (⅓ c)

50g pecans, chopped (½ c)

75g rolled oats (¾ c)

3 tablespoons sunflower seeds

2 tablespoons butter, melted

1 tablespoon honey or
   pure maple syrup

Chock-full of
**wholesome
goodness**

Savour the depth of
roasted hazelnut

Hazelnut and Chocolate Muffins

275g strong white bread flour

2 teaspoons baking powder

¼ teaspoon bicarbonate of soda

¼ teaspoon salt

75g dark or milk chocolate, chopped (⅓ c)

75g whole hazelnuts (½ c)

1 large egg

75–85g white granulated sugar (⅓ c)

100ml vegetable oil

100ml milk

200ml buttermilk*

2 tablespoons water

Optional topping: grated chocolate

**If you can't find a good thin
buttermilk, use a blend of milk and
whole milk yogurt, in equal portions.*

1   Preheat a conventional oven to 190°C (375°F), Gas Mark 5, fan oven 170°C. Prepare the muffin pan.

2   Spread whole hazelnuts on a baking sheet, and roast in a preheated oven about 5 minutes to bring out the flavour. Chop and set aside. Prepare both chopped and grated chocolate, and set aside.

3   In a large bowl, sift together flour, baking powder, bicarbonate of soda, and salt. Add chopped chocolate and hazelnuts.

4   In a medium-sized bowl, beat egg briskly with a fork. Add sugar, oil, milk, buttermilk, and water.

5   When the oven is ready, pour wet mixture into dry. With a metal spoon, mix lightly just until combined and no dry flour is visible, about 20 seconds. Do not beat or over stir.

6   Fill cups nearly full. Sprinkle with grated chocolate. Bake about 20 minutes until lightly browned. Makes 12.

Maple Walnut Muffins

225g strong white bread flour

3 teaspoons baking powder

¼ teaspoon salt

50g rolled oats (½ c)

100g butter (½ c)

50g walnuts or pecans, chopped (½ c)

1 large egg

250ml milk

100ml pure maple syrup

2–3 tablespoons white granulated sugar

Maple Syrup Glaze:

1 tablespoon soft butter

1 tablespoon maple syrup

50g icing sugar (½ c)

1. Preheat a conventional oven to 190°C (375°F), Gas Mark 5, fan oven 170°C. Prepare the muffin pan.

2. In a large bowl, sift together flour, baking powder, and salt. Add oats and butter. Cut in butter with a pastry blender (or rub lightly with fingers) until evenly distributed. Add nuts.

3. In a medium-sized bowl, beat egg briskly with a fork. Add milk, maple syrup, and sugar.

4. When the oven is ready, pour wet mixture into dry. With a metal spoon, mix lightly just until combined, about 20 seconds. Do not beat or over stir.

5. Fill cups nearly full. Bake about 20 minutes until golden brown. Stir glaze ingredients together until smooth, and spread thinly over the hot muffin tops. Makes 12.

A **special** treat

So simple,
so good

Oat Chocolate Chip Muffins

250g strong white bread flour

2½ teaspoons baking powder

¼ teaspoon bicarbonate of soda

¼ teaspoon salt

50g rolled oats (½ c)

75g chocolate chips (⅓ c)

1 large egg

75–85g light brown soft sugar (⅓ c)

100ml vegetable oil

300ml milk

1. Preheat a conventional oven to 190°C (375°F), Gas Mark 5, fan oven 170°C. Prepare the muffin pan.

2. In a large bowl, sift together flour, baking powder, bicarbonate of soda, and salt. Add oats and chocolate chips.

3. In a medium-sized bowl, beat egg briskly with a fork. Stir in sugar, oil, and milk.

4. When the oven is ready, pour all of wet mixture into dry. With a metal spoon, mix lightly just until combined and no dry flour is visible, about 20 seconds. Do not beat or over stir. Ignore the lumpy appearance of the batter.

5. Fill cups nearly full. Sprinkle tops with extra chocolate chips if desired. Bake about 20 minutes until lightly browned. Makes 12.

Oat Pear Muffins

250g strong white bread flour

2½ teaspoons baking powder

¼ teaspoon bicarbonate of soda

¼ teaspoon salt

50g rolled oats (½ c)

3 tablespoons chocolate chips

1 large egg

75–85g white granulated sugar (⅓ c)

100ml vegetable oil

200ml milk

3 tablespoons pear juice or water

200g finely chopped pear, fresh or
tinned (1 c)

1. Preheat a conventional oven to 190°C (375°F), Gas Mark 5, fan oven 170°C. Prepare the muffin pan.

2. In a large bowl, sift together flour, baking powder, bicarbonate of soda, and salt. Add oats and chocolate chips. (Chocolate can be omitted if preferred.)

3. In a medium-sized bowl, beat egg briskly with a fork. Add sugar, oil, milk, juice/water, and pear.

4. When the oven is ready, pour wet mixture into dry. Mix lightly with a metal spoon just until combined and no dry flour is visible, about 20 seconds. Do not beat or over stir.

5. Fill cups nearly full. Bake about 20 minutes until lightly browned. Makes 12.

Peanut Butter Oat Muffins

225g strong white bread flour

2½ teaspoons baking powder

¼ teaspoon bicarbonate of soda

¼ teaspoon salt

50g rolled oats (½ c)

3–4 tablespoons chocolate chips

1 large egg

75–85g white granulated sugar (⅓ c)

100ml vegetable oil

100g (6 tablespoons) peanut butter

300ml milk

Optional: 75g chopped dried apricots
(⅓ c) plus 2 tablespoons water

1. Preheat a conventional oven to 190°C (375°F), Gas Mark 5, fan oven 170°C. Prepare the muffin pan.

2. In a large bowl, sift together flour, baking powder, bicarbonate of soda, and salt. Add oats and chocolate chips. (Chocolate can be omitted if preferred.)

3. In a medium-sized bowl, beat egg briskly with a fork. Stir well after each addition: sugar, oil, peanut butter, and milk. (Add dried apricots and water, if using.) Continue stirring with a fork until the peanut butter is well distributed.

4. When the oven is ready, pour wet mixture into dry. Mix lightly with a metal spoon just until combined, about 20 seconds. Do not beat or over stir.

5. Fill cups nearly full. Bake about 20 minutes until golden brown. Makes 12.

FRUIT

Apple Harvest

Apple Layer

Apple Raspberry

Apple Spice

Banana

Banana Tropical

Blueberry

Blueberry Ricotta

Butternut Squash (Pumpkin)

Carrot Pineapple

Gingerbread Apple

Lemon

Lemon Cheesecake

Lemon-Filled

Mango

Orange

Orange Apricot

Orange Carrot Spice

Peach

Pear Ginger

Pineapple

Plum Orange

Raspberry Lemon

Raspberry and White Chocolate

Rhubarb Almond

Strawberry Rhubarb

Apple Harvest Muffins

250g strong white bread flour

3 teaspoons baking powder

¼ teaspoon salt

100g butter (½ c)

1 large egg

75–85g white granulated sugar (⅓ c)

200g finely chopped sweet red apple,
 such as Cox (1⅓ c)

200ml milk

100g raisins (⅔ c)

Topping: white granulated sugar

1. Preheat a conventional oven to 190°C (375°F), Gas Mark 5, fan oven 170°C. Prepare the muffin pan.

2. In a large bowl, sift together flour, baking powder, and salt. Cut in butter with a pastry blender (or rub in with fingers) until evenly distributed.

3. In a medium-sized bowl, beat egg briskly with a fork. Add sugar, apple, milk, and raisins.

4. When the oven is ready, pour wet mixture into dry. This batter is thick, so you will need to cut through the mixture with a metal spoon, lifting, folding, and combining as you turn the bowl. Mix only until no flour is visible, about 20 seconds.

5. Spoon into muffin cups. Sprinkle each top with a pinch of sugar. Bake about 20 minutes until golden brown. Makes 12.

A buttery muffin
loaded with fruit

A tasty **apple and cinnamon** filling

Apple Layer Muffins

250g strong white bread flour

3 teaspoons baking powder

¼ teaspoon salt

4 tablespoons wheat germ*

1 large egg

75g white granulated sugar (⅓ c)

100ml vegetable oil

250ml milk

2 tablespoons water

Filling:

150g thinly sliced sweet red apple (1 c)

1½ teaspoons ground cinnamon

1–2 tablespoons white granulated sugar

2 tablespoons butter, melted

*Flour can be substituted, if preferred.

1 Preheat a conventional oven to 190°C (375°F), Gas Mark 5, fan oven 170°C. Prepare the muffin pan.

2 Cut peeled apple into thin slices, and then cut the slices into approximate 1cm lengths. Combine cinnamon with 1–2 tablespoons sugar and mix with the apple. Add butter and set aside.

3 In a large bowl, sift together flour, baking powder, and salt. Add wheat germ (or flour).

4 In a medium-sized bowl, beat egg briskly with a fork. Add sugar, oil, milk, and water.

5 When the oven is ready, pour wet mixture into dry. With a metal spoon, mix lightly just until combined and no dry flour is visible, about 20 seconds. Do not beat or over stir.

6 Put a spoonful of batter into each cup to cover the base. Distribute the filling evenly, and finish with the remaining batter. Sprinkle each top with a pinch of sugar. Bake about 20 minutes until lightly browned. Makes 12.

Apple Raspberry Muffins

275g strong white bread flour

3 teaspoons baking powder

¼ teaspoon salt

1 large egg

75–85g white granulated sugar (⅓ c)

100ml vegetable oil

200ml milk

2 tablespoons water

125g coarsely chopped sweet red apple (¾ c)

125g raspberries, halved or quartered (¾ c);
  do not thaw if frozen

Crumble Topping:

50g rolled oats (½ c)

1–2 tablespoons light brown soft sugar

25g (2 tablespoons) butter, melted

1 Preheat a conventional oven to 190°C (375°F), Gas Mark 5, fan oven 170°C. Prepare the muffin pan.

2 Combine the topping ingredients. Stir well and set aside.

3 In a large bowl, sift together flour, baking powder, and salt.

4 In a medium-sized bowl, beat egg briskly with a fork. Add sugar, oil, milk, water, and apple. Prepare the berries but do not add them yet.

5 When the oven is ready, pour wet mixture into dry. With a metal spoon, mix lightly just until combined, about 20 seconds. Gently fold in the berries. Do not over stir. This batter should be fairly thick, as fruit releases juice during baking.

6 Fill cups nearly full. Sprinkle with topping. Bake about 20 minutes until lightly browned. Frozen fruit might require an extra 2–3 minutes. Makes 12.

Apple Spice Muffins

275g strong white bread flour

3 teaspoons baking powder

¼ teaspoon salt

2 teaspoons mixed spice*

1 large egg

75–85g white granulated sugar (⅓ c)

100ml vegetable oil

200ml milk

200g finely chopped sweet red apple,
   such as Cox (1⅓ c)

Topping:

1 tablespoon light brown soft sugar

50g walnuts, chopped (⅓ c)

*Mixed spice can be replaced with
1½ teaspoons ground cinnamon plus
¼ teaspoon each of ground nutmeg,
cloves, and ginger.

1   Preheat a conventional oven to 190°C (375°F), Gas Mark 5, fan oven 170°C. Prepare the muffin pan.

2   Combine topping ingredients and set aside. (Note: Nuts can be omitted or added to the batter if preferred.)

3   In a large bowl, sift together flour, baking powder, salt, and spice.

4   In a medium-sized bowl, beat egg briskly with a fork. Stir in sugar, oil, milk, and apple.

5   When the oven is ready, pour wet mixture into dry. With a metal spoon, mix lightly just until combined, about 20 seconds. Do not over stir. The batter will be fairly thick, as apple releases juice during baking.

6   Fill cups nearly full. Sprinkle with topping. Bake about 20 minutes until lightly browned. Makes 12.

Banana Muffins

275g strong white bread flour

2 teaspoons baking powder

½ teaspoon bicarbonate of soda

¼ teaspoon salt

1 large egg

75–85g white granulated sugar (⅓ c)

100ml vegetable oil

300ml ripe banana purée (about 3 large)

150ml milk

1–2 tablespoons water*

Optional: 50g chocolate chips (¼ c) or
  chopped walnuts (½ c)

**Tip: Ripe bananas can be frozen in
an air-tight container or bag for future
use. These will be quite wet when
thawed, so the smaller amount of
water should be used.*

1 Preheat a conventional oven to 190°C (375°F), Gas Mark 5, fan oven 170°C. Prepare the muffin pan.

2 Purée bananas thoroughly until smooth, using either an electric blender or potato masher. Measure 300ml.

3 In a large bowl, sift together flour, baking powder, bicarbonate of soda, and salt. (Add chocolate chips if using.)

4 In a medium-sized bowl, beat egg briskly with a fork. Stir in sugar, oil, banana purée, milk, and water.

5 When the oven is ready, pour wet mixture into dry. (Add nuts if using.) With a metal spoon, mix lightly just until combined and no dry flour is visible, about 20 seconds. Do not beat or over stir.

6 Fill cups nearly full. Bake about 20 minutes until lightly browned. Makes 12.

An **exotic blend** with pineapple and coconut

Banana Tropical Muffins

275g strong white bread flour

2 teaspoons baking powder

½ teaspoon bicarbonate of soda

¼ teaspoon salt

1 large egg

75–85g white granulated sugar (⅓ c)

100ml vegetable oil

150ml ripe banana purée (2 medium)

150ml milk

150g pineapple (4 tinned slices), chopped (⅔ c)

2 tablespoons pineapple juice or water

Topping: desiccated coconut

1 Preheat a conventional oven to 190°C (375°F), Gas Mark 5, fan oven 170°C. Prepare the muffin pan.

2 Purée bananas thoroughly until smooth, using either a potato masher or an electric blender. Measure 150ml.

3 In a large bowl, sift together flour, baking powder, bicarbonate of soda, and salt.

4 In a medium-sized bowl, beat egg briskly with a fork. Stir in sugar, oil, banana purée, milk, pineapple, and juice.

5 When the oven is up to temperature, pour wet mixture into dry. Mix lightly with a metal spoon just until combined and no dry flour is visible, about 20 seconds. Do not beat or over stir.

6 Fill cups nearly full. Sprinkle generously with coconut. Bake about 20 minutes until golden brown. Makes 12.

Blueberry Muffins

300g strong white bread flour

3 teaspoons baking powder

¼ teaspoon salt

1 large egg

75–85g white granulated sugar (⅓ c)

100ml vegetable oil

250ml milk

1 tablespoon water

100g finely chopped sweet red apple (⅔ c)*

25g (2 tablespoons) butter, melted

150–200g blueberries (1–1⅓ c); do not
thaw if frozen

*Apple adds natural sweetness and
a moist texture. To make these without
apple, simply substitute an extra
2 tablespoons water.*

1   Preheat a conventional oven to 190°C (375°F), Gas Mark 5,
fan oven 170°C. Prepare the muffin pan.

2   In a large bowl, sift together flour, baking powder, and salt.

3   In a medium-sized bowl, beat egg briskly with a fork.
Add sugar, oil, milk, water, apple, and butter.

4   When the oven is ready, pour wet mixture into dry. Using
a metal spoon, mix lightly just until combined and no dry
flour is visible, about 20 seconds. Gently fold in the berries.
Do not over stir.

5   Fill cups nearly full. Sprinkle each top with a pinch of sugar,
if desired. Bake about 20 minutes until lightly browned.
Frozen fruit might require an extra 2–3 minutes.

A classic with
a **new twist**

Deliciously moreish

Blueberry Ricotta Muffins

275g strong white bread flour

3 teaspoons baking powder

¼ teaspoon salt

1 large egg

75g white granulated sugar (⅓ c)

100ml vegetable oil

250ml milk

1 tablespoon lemon juice, at final mixing

Filling:

125g ricotta cheese

2 tablespoons white granulated sugar

125g blueberries (¾ c); do not thaw
  if frozen

1. Preheat a conventional oven to 190°C (375°F), Gas Mark 5, fan oven 170°C. Prepare the muffin pan.

2. Combine ricotta cheese and 2 tablespoons sugar. Keep blueberries separate.

3. In a large bowl, sift together flour, baking powder, and salt.

4. In a medium-sized bowl, beat egg briskly with a fork. Stir in sugar, oil, and milk. Prepare lemon juice but do not add until the final mixing.

5. When the oven is ready, add lemon juice to the wet mixture and then immediately pour wet into dry. With a metal spoon, mix lightly just until combined and no dry flour is visible, about 20 seconds. Do not over stir.

6. Put a spoonful of batter into each muffin cup to cover the base. Distribute ricotta filling, dropping it in two smaller clumps per cup rather than one large clump. Distribute berries. Top with remaining batter, and sprinkle with a pinch of sugar if desired. Bake about 20 minutes until lightly browned. Frozen fruit might require an extra 2–3 minutes. Makes 12.

Butternut Squash Muffins

250g strong white bread flour

2 teaspoons baking powder

1 teaspoon bicarbonate of soda

¼ teaspoon salt

2 teaspoons ground cinnamon

½ teaspoon ground ginger

¼ teaspoon ground cloves

1 large egg

75–85g white granulated sugar (⅓ c)

100ml vegetable oil

150ml milk

2 tablespoons water (use 4 tablespoons
with tinned pumpkin)

250ml butternut squash purée, or
tinned pumpkin

Optional: 50g chopped walnuts (½ c)

For Cream Cheese Icing, see page 79.

1   Peel and cut up a medium-sized squash. Discard pulp. Place chunks in a saucepan of boiling water and simmer about 20 minutes until tender. Discard water. Spread squash on a baking sheet to cool completely, to reduce excess moisture. Mash to make a purée, and measure 250ml. Tinned pumpkin is thicker than fresh cooked squash.

2   Preheat a conventional oven to 190°C (375°F), Gas Mark 5, fan oven 170°C. Prepare the muffin pan.

3   In a large bowl, sift together flour, baking powder, bicarbonate of soda, salt, and spices.

4   In a medium-sized bowl, beat egg briskly with a fork. Stir in sugar, oil, milk, water, and purée.

5   When the oven is ready, pour wet mixture into dry. (Add nuts if using.) With a metal spoon, mix lightly just until combined and no dry flour is visible, about 20 seconds. Do not beat or over stir.

6   Fill cups nearly full. Bake about 20 minutes until done. Makes 12.

7   Spread Cream Cheese Icing on cooled muffins.

Tinned pumpkin is a **simple substitute**

Moist and
lightly spiced

Carrot Pineapple Muffins

250g strong white bread flour

2 teaspoons baking powder

½ teaspoon bicarbonate of soda

¼ teaspoon salt

2½ teaspoons ground cinnamon

¼ teaspoon ground nutmeg

1 large egg

75–85g white granulated sugar (⅓ c)

100ml vegetable oil

100ml milk

200g finely grated carrot (1 c)

150g pineapple, chopped (⅔ c)*

3 tablespoons pineapple juice*

Cream Cheese Icing:

50g full fat cream cheese

1 tablespoon soft butter (not melted)

100g icing sugar (¾ c)

¼ teaspoon vanilla extract

1 Preheat a conventional oven to 190°C (375°F), Gas Mark 5, fan oven 170°C. Prepare the muffin pan.

2 Prepare carrots. Fine grating is necessary for carrot juice to be released into the batter during baking.

3 In a large bowl, sift together flour, baking powder, bicarbonate of soda, salt, and spices.

4 In a medium-sized bowl, beat egg briskly with a fork. Add sugar, oil, milk, carrot, pineapple, and juice.

5 When the oven is ready, pour wet mixture into dry. Mix lightly with a metal spoon just until combined and no dry flour is visible, about 20 seconds. The batter will be quite thick.

6 Spoon into cases and bake about 20 minutes until lightly browned. Makes 12.

7 Stir icing ingredients together until smooth.

If preferred, pineapple and juice can be omitted. Substitute 100ml water in total.

Gingerbread Apple Muffins

250g strong white bread flour

½ teaspoon baking powder

1 teaspoon bicarbonate of soda

¼ teaspoon salt

2 teaspoons ground ginger

1 teaspoon ground cinnamon

¼ teaspoon ground nutmeg

1 large egg

75–85g light brown soft sugar (⅓ c)

100ml vegetable oil

2 tablespoons treacle or light molasses

100ml milk

250ml applesauce (see adjacent)

75g raisins or sultanas (½ c)

1   Preheat a conventional oven to 190°C (375°F), Gas Mark 5, fan oven 170°C. Prepare the muffin pan.

2   Peel and slice 2 medium eating apples, such as Granny Smith or Cox, into a saucepan. Add 200ml water, cover, and bring to the boil. Reduce heat and simmer until the apple is soft and breaking down, about 5 minutes. Mash to make a wet lumpy purée. Cool and measure 250ml for the recipe. Note: Tart cooking apples such as Bramley are not recommended as they create excessive bubbling in the batter, causing the muffins to rise quickly and then sink.

3   In a large bowl, sift together flour, baking powder, bicarbonate of soda, salt, and spices.

4   In a separate bowl, beat egg briskly with a fork. Stir well after each addition: sugar, oil, treacle, milk, cooled applesauce, and raisins.

5   When the oven is ready, pour wet mixture into dry. Using a metal spoon, mix lightly just until combined and no dry flour is visible, about 20 seconds. Do not beat or over stir.

6   Fill cups nearly full. Bake about 20 minutes until done. Makes 12.

A **delicious duo** of dried and fresh mango

Double orange for **double flavour**

Orange Muffins

275g strong white bread flour

2 teaspoons baking powder

¼ teaspoon bicarbonate of soda

¼ teaspoon salt

1 large egg

75–85g white granulated sugar (⅓ c)

1 tablespoon finely grated orange zest
  (of 3 firm juice oranges)

100ml vegetable oil

100ml milk

150ml fresh orange juice, at final mixing

150g tinned mandarin orange
  segments, drained and sliced (⅔ c)*

*Tinned mandarin segments are
sweeter and less fibrous than fresh.
If you prefer to omit them, simply
substitute 2 tablespoons water.*

1   Preheat a conventional oven to 190°C (375°F), Gas Mark 5, fan oven 170°C. Prepare the muffin pan.

2   In a large bowl, sift together flour, baking powder, bicarbonate of soda, and salt.

3   In a medium-sized bowl, beat egg briskly with a fork. Stir in sugar, zest, oil, and milk. (Add dates if using.) Prepare orange juice and mandarin segments but do not add until the final mixing.

4   When the oven is ready, add juice and mandarins (or water) to the wet mixture. Pour wet into dry, and mix lightly with a metal spoon just until combined, about 20 seconds.

5   Spoon immediately into cups. Bake about 20 minutes until golden brown. Makes 12.

Orange Glazed Muffins   Combine 60g icing sugar (½ c), ¼ teaspoon finely grated orange zest, and 2¼ teaspoons orange juice. Spread thinly over hot tops.

Orange Date Muffins   Add 50g soft dates, chopped (⅓ c). If the dates are hard, soak first in hot water for 10 minutes.

Orange Apricot Muffins

275g strong white bread flour

2 teaspoons baking powder

¼ teaspoon bicarbonate of soda

¼ teaspoon salt

1 large egg

75–85g white granulated sugar (⅓ c)

100ml vegetable oil

2 teaspoons finely grated orange zest
(of 2 firm juice oranges)

100ml milk

50ml water

175g chopped apricots, fresh or
tinned (1 c)

100ml fresh orange juice, at final mixing

1 Preheat a conventional oven to 190°C (375°F), Gas Mark 5, fan oven 170°C. Prepare the muffin pan.

2 In a large bowl, sift together flour, baking powder, bicarbonate of soda, and salt.

3 In a medium-sized bowl, beat egg briskly with a fork. Add sugar, oil, zest, milk, water, and apricots. Prepare orange juice but do not add until the final mixing.

4 When the oven has reached the correct temperature, add orange juice to the wet mixture and then immediately pour wet into dry. Mix lightly with a metal spoon just until combined, about 20 seconds. Do not beat or over stir. This batter will be fairly thick.

5 Spoon into cups. Bake about 20 minutes until golden brown. Makes 12.

Sunshine
in a muffin

An **enticing** blend

Orange Carrot Spice Muffins

275g strong white bread flour

2 teaspoons baking powder

½ teaspoon bicarbonate of soda

¼ teaspoon salt

½ teaspoon ground cinnamon

¼ teaspoon ground cloves

¼ teaspoon ground nutmeg

1 large egg

75g white granulated sugar (⅓ c)

100ml vegetable oil

1 teaspoon finely grated orange zest

100ml milk

2 tablespoons water

150g carrot, finely grated (¾ c)

100ml fresh orange juice, at the final mixing

Topping:

2 tablespoons light brown soft sugar

1 tablespoon butter, melted

50g pecans or walnuts, chopped (½ c)

1. Preheat a conventional oven to 190°C (375°F), Gas Mark 5, fan oven 170°C. Prepare the muffin pan.

2. Combine the topping ingredients and set aside.

3. In a large bowl, sift together flour, baking powder, bicarbonate of soda, salt, and spices.

4. In a medium-sized bowl, beat egg briskly with a fork. Stir in sugar, oil, zest, milk, water, and carrot. Prepare the orange juice but do not add until the final mixing.

5. When the oven is up to temperature, add the orange juice to the wet ingredients and then pour wet into dry. With a metal spoon, mix lightly just until combined and no dry flour is visible, about 20 seconds. Do not over stir.

6. Fill cups nearly full. Distribute topping. Bake about 20 minutes until lightly browned. Makes 12.

Peach Muffins

275g strong white bread flour

2 teaspoons baking powder

¼ teaspoon bicarbonate of soda

¼ teaspoon salt

1 large egg

75–85g white granulated sugar (⅓ c)

100ml vegetable oil

200ml buttermilk*

100ml milk

½ teaspoon almond extract or cinnamon

Fruit Filling:

250g ripe peaches or nectarines,
   thinly sliced (1⅓ c)

2 tablespoons light brown soft sugar

1 tablespoon butter, melted

*If you can't find a good thin buttermilk,
substitute a blend of milk and whole
milk yogurt, in equal parts.*

1   Preheat a conventional oven to 190°C (375°F), Gas Mark 5, fan oven 170°C. Prepare the muffin pan.

2   Prepare the filling: slice fruit thinly and then cut into shorter pieces. Mix with brown sugar and butter, and set aside.

3   In a large bowl, sift together flour, baking powder, bicarbonate of soda, and salt. (Add cinnamon if using.)

4   In a medium-sized bowl, beat egg briskly with a fork. Add sugar, oil, buttermilk, and milk. (Add almond extract if using.)

5   When the oven is ready, pour wet mixture into dry. Mix lightly with a metal spoon just until combined, about 20 seconds. Do not beat or over stir. The batter will be fairly thick.

6   Put a spoonful of batter into each cup to cover the base. Distribute the filling, and top with remaining batter. Sprinkle a pinch of sugar over each top if desired. Bake about 20 minutes until lightly browned. Makes 12.

A **fresh take** on a modern classic

Raspberry and White Chocolate Muffins

275g strong white bread flour

3 teaspoons baking powder

¼ teaspoon salt

100g white chocolate, coarsely chopped
  (½ c)

1 large egg

75–85g white granulated sugar (⅓ c)

100ml vegetable oil

200ml milk

2 tablespoons water

100g finely chopped sweet red apple
  (⅔ c)

100g raspberries, quartered (¾ c);
  do not thaw if frozen

Decoration: 50g extra raspberries
  (about 10), quartered

1 Preheat a conventional oven to 190°C (375°F), Gas Mark 5, fan oven 170°C. Prepare the muffin pan.

2 In a large bowl, sift together flour, baking powder, and salt. Add white chocolate.

3 In a medium-sized bowl, beat egg briskly with a fork. Add sugar, oil, milk, water, and apple. Prepare the berries in two separate piles, but do not add them to the batter. Instead they will be added in layers to ensure an even balance with the subtle chocolate flavour.

4 When the oven is ready, pour wet mixture into dry. With a metal spoon, mix lightly just until combined, about 20 seconds. Do not over stir. This batter should be quite thick, as fruit releases juice during baking.

5 Put a spoonful of batter into each cup to cover the base. Distribute 100g raspberries evenly, and finish with remaining batter. Top with 50g extra raspberry pieces. Bake about 20 minutes until lightly browned. Frozen fruit might require an extra 2–3 minutes. Makes 12.

Rhubarb Almond Muffins

275g strong white bread flour

2 teaspoons baking powder

¼ teaspoon bicarbonate of soda

¼ teaspoon salt

1 large egg

75–85g white granulated sugar (⅓ c)

75ml vegetable oil

1 teaspoon almond extract

150ml sour cream (cultured)

100ml milk

2 tablespoons water

200g finely chopped fresh rhubarb* (1⅓ c);
   do not thaw if frozen

Topping:

50g chopped almonds (⅓ c)

2 tablespoons soft brown sugar

*For tinned rhubarb, add an extra
2 tablespoons water.*

1 Preheat a conventional oven to 190°C (375°F), Gas Mark 5, fan oven 170°C. Prepare the muffin pan.

2 Combine the topping ingredients, and set aside.

3 In a large bowl, sift together flour, baking powder, bicarbonate of soda, and salt.

4 In a medium-sized bowl, beat egg briskly with a fork. Stir in sugar, oil, almond extract, sour cream, milk, water, and rhubarb. (The rhubarb needs to be finely chopped to release juice into the batter.)

5 When the oven is ready, pour wet mixture into dry. With a metal spoon, mix lightly just until combined, about 20 seconds. Do not beat or over stir. The batter will be fairly thick.

6 Fill cups nearly full. Sprinkle with topping. Bake about 20 minutes until lightly browned. Frozen fruit might require an extra 2–3 minutes. Makes 12.

A **delectable**
sour cream muffin

A **blissful** blend

Strawberry Rhubarb Muffins

275g strong white bread flour

3 teaspoons baking powder

¼ teaspoon salt

1 large egg

75–85g white granulated sugar (⅓ c)

100ml vegetable oil

½ teaspoon lemon zest

200ml milk

2 tablespoons water

1 tablespoon lemon juice, at final mixing

Fruit Filling:

150g rhubarb, chopped (1¼ c)

150g strawberries, chopped (1 c)

2 tablespoons white granulated sugar

1½ teaspoons cornflour (cornstarch)

2 tablespoons cold water

1 tablespoon butter

1 Make the filling at least 30 minutes in advance to allow for cooling. Place rhubarb and strawberries in a small saucepan with sugar, cornflour, and water. Stir constantly over low heat for about 3 minutes until juices are released and thickened. Stir in butter. Transfer to a bowl to cool completely, in the fridge if possible.

2 Preheat a conventional oven to 190°C (375°F), Gas Mark 5, fan oven 170°C. Prepare the muffin pan.

3 In a large bowl, sift together flour, baking powder, and salt.

4 In a medium-sized bowl, beat egg briskly with a fork. Stir in sugar, oil, zest, milk, and water. Prepare the lemon juice but do not add until the final mixing.

5 When the oven is ready, add lemon juice to the wet mixture and then immediately pour wet into dry. With a metal spoon, mix lightly just until combined, about 20 seconds. Do not over stir.

6 Put a spoonful of batter into each cup to cover the base. Distribute filling, and finish with remaining batter. Bake about 20 minutes until golden brown. Makes 12.

BRAN

Apricot Blueberry Bran
Orange Date Bran
Sultana Bran
Yogurt Bran

Apricot Blueberry Bran Muffins

275g strong white bread flour

2 teaspoons baking powder

¼ teaspoon bicarbonate of soda

¼ teaspoon salt

1 large egg

75–85g white granulated sugar (⅓ c)

100ml vegetable oil

200ml buttermilk*

100ml milk

2 tablespoons water

25g wheat bran (½ c)

125g chopped apricots, fresh or tinned (⅔ c)

100g blueberries (⅔ c); do not thaw
    frozen berries

*If you can't find a good thin buttermilk,
use a blend of milk and whole milk yogurt,
in equal parts.

1   Preheat a conventional oven to 190°C (375°F), Gas Mark 5, fan oven 170°C. Prepare the muffin pan.

2   In a large bowl, sift together flour, baking powder, bicarbonate of soda, and salt.

3   In a medium-sized bowl, beat egg briskly with a fork. Stir in sugar, oil, buttermilk, milk, water, bran, and apricots.

4   When the oven is ready, pour wet mixture into dry. With a metal spoon, mix lightly just until combined, about 20 seconds. Fold in berries during the final strokes. The batter will be fairly thick.

5   Fill cups nearly full. Bake about 20 minutes until lightly browned. Frozen fruit might require an extra 2–3 minutes. Makes 12.

Light, wholesome, **and fruity**

Orange Date Bran Muffins

250g strong white bread flour

2½ teaspoons baking powder

½ teaspoon bicarbonate of soda

¼ teaspoon salt

1 large egg

75–85g light brown soft sugar (⅓ c)

100ml vegetable oil

1 teaspoon finely grated orange zest

25g wheat bran (½ c)

4 tablespoons wheat germ*

250ml milk

2 tablespoons water

150g soft dried dates, chopped (1 c)

3 tablespoons fresh orange juice

If wheat germ is unavailable, increase wheat bran to 50g (1 cup) total.

1. Preheat a conventional oven to 190°C (375°F), Gas Mark 5, fan oven 170°C. Prepare the muffin pan.

2. If the dates are hard, soak them first in hot water for about 10 minutes before chopping.

3. In a large bowl, sift together flour, baking powder, bicarbonate of soda, and salt.

4. In a medium-sized bowl, beat egg briskly with a fork. Add sugar, oil, zest, bran, wheat germ, milk, water, dates, and orange juice.

5. When the oven is ready, pour wet mixture into dry. With a metal spoon, mix lightly just until combined and no dry flour is visible, about 20 seconds. Do not beat or over stir.

6. Fill cups nearly full. Bake about 20 minutes until lightly browned. Makes 12. Bran muffins are traditionally eaten split and buttered.

Sultana Bran Muffins

250g strong white bread flour

2½ teaspoons baking powder

¼ teaspoon bicarbonate of soda

¼ teaspoon salt

1 large egg

75–85g light brown soft sugar (⅓ c)

2 tablespoons treacle, light molasses, or honey

100ml vegetable oil

300ml milk

2 tablespoons water

50g natural wheat bran (1 c)

75g sultanas or raisins (½ c)

1 Preheat a conventional oven to 190°C (375°F), Gas Mark 5, fan oven 170°C. Prepare the muffin pan.

2 Soak the dried fruit for 10 minutes in hot water, and drain before using.

3 In a large bowl, sift together flour, baking powder, bicarbonate of soda, and salt.

4 In a medium-sized bowl, beat egg briskly with a fork. Stir well after each addition: sugar, treacle, oil, milk, water, bran, and sultanas.

5 When the oven is ready, pour wet mixture into dry. With a metal spoon, mix lightly just until combined and no dry flour is visible, about 20 seconds. Do not over stir.

6 Spoon into muffin cups. Bake about 20 minutes until lightly browned. Makes 12.

Great for **breakfast** or **snack**

Yogurt Bran Muffins

250g strong white bread flour

2 teaspoons baking powder

¼ teaspoon bicarbonate of soda

¼ teaspoon salt

1 large egg

75–85g light brown soft sugar (⅓ c)

100ml vegetable oil

150ml whole milk yogurt

250ml milk

50g wheat bran (1 c)

75g sultanas, raisins, or dried
cranberries (½ c)

1 Preheat a conventional oven to 190°C (375°F), Gas Mark 5,
fan oven 170°C. Prepare the muffin pan.

2 In a large bowl, sift together flour, baking powder,
bicarbonate of soda, and salt.

3 In a medium-sized bowl, beat egg briskly with a fork. Stir
well after each addition: sugar, oil, yogurt, milk, bran, and
dried fruit.

4 When the oven is ready, pour wet mixture into dry. With a
metal spoon, mix lightly just until combined and no dry flour
is visible, about 20 seconds. Do not beat or over stir.

5 Fill cups nearly full. Bake about 20 minutes until lightly
browned. Makes 12.

SAVOURY

Apple and Cheese
Cheddar Cheese
Feta and Leek
Gruyère and Onion

Apple Cheese Muffins

275g strong white bread flour

2 teaspoons baking powder

¼ teaspoon bicarbonate of soda

¼ teaspoon salt

100g smoked Cheddar,* coarsely grated (1 c)

1 large egg

1–2 tablespoons white granulated sugar

75ml vegetable oil

250ml milk

2 tablespoons water

100g finely chopped sweet red apple (⅔ c)

Topping: extra cheese

Or mature Cheddar.

1. Preheat a conventional oven to 190°C (375°F), Gas Mark 5, fan oven 170°C. Prepare the muffin pan.

2. In a large bowl, sift together flour, baking powder, bicarbonate of soda, and salt. Add cheese.

3. In a medium-sized bowl, beat egg briskly with a fork. Stir in sugar, oil, milk, water, and apple.

4. When the oven is ready, pour wet mixture into dry. With a metal spoon, mix lightly just until combined and no dry flour is visible, about 20 seconds. The batter will be quite thick.

5. Spoon into muffin cups. Sprinkle with extra cheese. Bake about 20 minutes until golden brown. Makes 12.

Perfect for a
savoury snack

Simple and **satisfying**

Cheddar Cheese Muffins

275g strong white bread flour

2 teaspoons baking powder

¼ teaspoon bicarbonate of soda

¼ teaspoon salt

100g Cheddar, coarsely grated (1 c)

1 large egg

1–2 tablespoons white granulated sugar

100ml vegetable oil

100ml whole milk yogurt

250ml milk

3 tablespoons finely chopped chives
   or spring onion

Topping: extra cheese

1   Preheat a conventional oven to 190°C (375°F), Gas Mark 5, fan oven 170°C. Prepare the muffin pan.

2   In a large bowl, sift together flour, baking powder, bicarbonate of soda, and salt. Add cheese.

3   In a medium-sized bowl, beat egg briskly with a fork. Add sugar, oil, yogurt, milk, and chives.

4   When the oven is ready, pour wet mixture into dry. Mix lightly with a metal spoon just until combined and no dry flour is visible, about 20 seconds. Do not over stir. The batter will be quite thick.

5   Spoon into muffin cups. Sprinkle with extra cheese. Bake about 20 minutes until golden brown. Makes 12.

Feta and Leek Muffins

275g strong white bread flour

2½ teaspoons baking powder

¼ teaspoon bicarbonate of soda

¼ teaspoon salt

1 large egg

1–2 tablespoons white granulated sugar

75ml vegetable oil

250ml milk

50ml water

200g chopped leeks (2 c)

2 tablespoons oil for sautéing leeks

100g feta cheese, rinsed and chopped (¾ c)

Optional: 40g pine nuts (¼ c)

Topping: extra cheese or pine nuts

1   Preheat a conventional oven to 190°C (375°F), Gas Mark 5, fan oven 170°C. Prepare the muffin pan.

2   Sauté leeks in 2 tablespoons oil over low heat for about 5 minutes, stirring frequently until soft but not browned.

3   If using pine nuts, spread them on a baking sheet and roast in a preheated oven for 1 minute. Do not scorch.

4   In a large bowl, sift together flour, baking powder, bicarbonate of soda, and salt. (Add pine nuts if using.)

5   In a separate bowl, beat egg briskly with a fork. Stir in sugar, oil, milk, water, sautéed leeks, and feta.

6   When the oven is ready, pour wet mixture into dry. Mix lightly with a metal spoon just until combined, about 20 seconds. Do not over stir. The batter will be quite thick.

7   Spoon into muffin cups. Sprinkle with topping. Bake about 20 minutes until lightly browned. Makes 12.

Photo: page 118, right

Gruyère and Onion Muffins

275g strong white bread flour

2½ teaspoons baking powder

¼ teaspoon bicarbonate of soda

¼ teaspoon salt

100g Gruyère,* coarsely grated (1 c)

1 large egg

1–2 tablespoons white granulated sugar

75ml vegetable oil

250ml milk

50ml water

3 medium white onions, sliced thinly

2 tablespoons oil for sautéing onions

Topping: extra cheese

*Other hard cheeses can be used,
such as Cheddar.*

1 Preheat a conventional oven to 190°C (375°F), Gas Mark 5, fan oven 170°C. Prepare the muffin pan.

2 Sauté onions in 2 tablespoons oil over low heat for 10–15 minutes, until soft and golden. Stir frequently to prevent scorching. Allow to cool.

3 In a large bowl, sift together flour, baking powder, bicarbonate of soda, and salt. Add cheese.

4 In a medium-sized bowl, beat egg briskly with a fork. Add sugar, 75ml oil, milk, water, and sautéed onions.

5 When the oven is ready, pour wet mixture into dry. Using a metal spoon, mix lightly just until combined and no dry flour is visible, about 20 seconds. Do not over stir. The batter will be thick and lumpy.

6 Spoon into muffin cups. Sprinkle tops with extra cheese. Bake about 20 minutes until golden brown. Makes 12.

GLUTEN- AND WHEAT-FREE BAKING

The terms 'gluten-free' and 'wheat-free' are often confused. A person diagnosed with coeliac disease is unable to eat any foods containing gluten, including wheat, oats, barley, and rye, while someone who is wheat intolerant might be able to include other grains in their diet.

On their own, non-wheat flours produce a dense powdery texture that practically dissolves in the mouth, leaving nothing to chew. Surprisingly, by combining some of these flours, there is a marked improvement which can be enhanced further by adding extra egg to bind it together. For top quality gluten-free baking, an extra ingredient called xanthan gum will give that tender chewiness that makes baked goods so enjoyable to eat. Xanthan gum is a natural product, commonly used in foods such as salad dressings.

Nowadays gluten-free flour mixes are available in most supermarkets. For those who are unable to access those products, I am including instructions for the gluten-free flour mix that I developed in 2001 for the third edition of *Muffins*.

Remember to use two eggs instead of one. Also be prepared to adjust the amount of liquid. Gluten-free muffin batter needs to be quite 'sloppy' as rice flour is more absorbent than wheat flour.

The following quantity will make 275g gluten-free flour. Sift the mixture twice to distribute the xanthan gum evenly.

200g rice flour
(ideally a mix of white and brown)

50g potato flour
(potato starch)

25g tapioca flour
(not granules)
or cornflour
(that is cornstarch, not cornmeal)

1 teaspoon xanthan gum

METRIC CONVERSIONS

All conversions are approximate. These two tables are *not* for converting weight to volume.

Weight (for scales)			Volume (for jug)	
METRIC (GRAMS)	IMPERIAL (OUNCES)		METRIC (MILLILITRES)	AMERICAN (CUPS AND TABLESPOONS)
300g	10.5 oz		250ml	1 cup
275g	10 oz		200ml	¾ cup + 2 tablespoons
250g	9 oz		175ml	¾ cup
225g	8 oz		150ml	⅔ cup
200g	7 oz		125ml	½ cup
175g	6 oz		100ml	⅓ cup + 2 tablespoons
150g	5 oz		75ml	⅓ cup
125g	4.5 oz		50ml	¼ cup
100g	3.5 oz		15ml	1 level tablespoon
75g	2.5 oz		5ml	1 level teaspoon
50g	2 oz			

FLOUR VOLUME MEASURES

In this edition, British strong flour, also known as bread flour, is the flour of choice. It has a gluten (protein) content of approximately 13% which is similar to American all-purpose flour. These two types of flour can be used interchangeably for these recipes.

For best results in baking, weigh scales are strongly recommended. The volume measure of flour fluctuates according to milling, sifting, and settling, and this inaccuracy can have a significant effect on batter consistency and final quality. If you still want to measure flour by volume, be sure to use proper dry measuring cups that can be levelled off with a straight edge. A measuring jug is too inaccurate.

All-purpose flour has a slightly finer milled texture than British strong flour which results in a small difference when measuring by volume, as seen in the table.

A note for British bakers: plain flour and self-raising flour are *not* interchangeable with strong bread flour. Should you choose to use plain or self-raising flour for these recipes, you will need to make adjustments to the amount of liquid. Please refer to the notes on page 12.

The following chart uses these measures:
1 American cup (c) = 240ml
1 tablespoon = 15ml

WEIGHT	American all-purpose flour VOLUME	British strong bread flour VOLUME
300g	2 c + 3 tablespoons	2¼ c
275g	2 c	2 c + 1 tablespoon
250g	1¾ c + 1 tablespoon	1¾ c + 2 tablespoons
225g	1½ c + 2 tablespoons	1½ c + 3 tablespoons